Learn from the Greats and Become Greater

102 Empowering Quotes to Create A Success Mindset

By Michelle Lynch

Learn from the Greats and Become Greater
102 Empowering Quotes to Create A Success Mindset

By Michelle Lynch

Printed by Amazon KDP
Created and published through the Publishing to Profit Training Quote Book Generator

Printed in the United States of America
10 9 8 7 6 5 4 3 2

Introduction

Have you ever heard a story, or an idea, or maybe just an old saying that struck a nerve inside you and made you feel like you could do anything; whatever you set your mind to?

That has happened to me many times. And in those moments, I feel invincible. Like I am just one step away from everything that is possible for me in this life. I feel tuned in and aligned. Everything unfolds as it should and I feel like nothing stands in my way.

I have also had moments of self-doubt, when life feels like a struggle and I don't know how I am going to get to where I want to go. When that happens, I look everywhere for evidence that someone, somewhere, has been there before. Someone has come up against an obstacle just like mine and overcame it. If I can discover how they got through it or something in their words shows me what I have overlooked, I will be better for it. And I, too, can prevail.

All I need in those moments is a little bit of light, a shimmer of hope, a knowing somewhere inside me that if someone else did it, it can be done. When I find that inspiration, which I always do, I am back on track. Sometimes fast and sometimes slow, either way I still press on, ready to jump in again and go for it.

I decided to put together this collection of empowering quotes for anyone who has had a time in their life when they just needed to remember who they really are and what they really want. And for all of us to know that we are capable of great things. Others have come before us and paved a way. We can do the same, or even better.

May you find your bliss and live there always,
Michelle Lynch

"The most important thing for me to remember is that life is not happening TO me. I'm creating it. I don't just have to wait and see what fate will bring. With my thoughts and actions, in every moment, I'm bringing it." -Michelle Lynch

Beginning Your Day

What does this quote mean to me today?

_____
_____
_____

How will I apply this quote today?

_____
_____
_____

Who else needs to hear this quote today?

_____
_____
_____

At the End of Your Day

What will I do differently going forward?

_____
_____
_____

Knowing what I now know, what I am grateful for today?

_____
_____
_____

"Our deepest fear is not that we are inadequate. It is that we are powerful beyond our measure. It is our light, not our darkness that most frightens us. We ask ourselves, 'Who am I to be brilliant, gorgeous, talented, fabulous?' Actually, who are you not to be? Your playing small does not serve the world. There is nothing enlightened about shrinking so that other people won't feel insecure around you." -Marianne Williamson

Beginning Your Day

What does this quote mean to me today?

_____
_____
_____

How will I apply this quote today?

_____
_____
_____

Who else needs to hear this quote today?

_____
_____
_____

At the End of Your Day

What will I do differently going forward?

_____
_____
_____

Knowing what I now know, what I am grateful for today?

_____
_____
_____

"True understanding is to see the events of life in this way: 'You are here for my benefit, though rumor paints you otherwise.' And everything is turned to one's advantage when he greets a situation like this: You are the very thing I was looking for. Truly whatever arises in life is the right material to bring about your growth and the growth of those around you." -Marcus Aurelius

Beginning Your Day
What does this quote mean to me today?

_____
_____
_____

How will I apply this quote today?

_____
_____
_____

Who else needs to hear this quote today?

_____
_____
_____

At the End of Your Day
What will I do differently going forward?

_____
_____
_____

Knowing what I now know, what I am grateful for today?

_____
_____
_____

"Do the one thing you think you cannot do. Fail at it. Try again. Do better the second time. The only people who never tumble are those who never mount the high wire. This is your moment. Own it." -Oprah Winfrey

Beginning Your Day

What does this quote mean to me today?

_____
_____
_____

How will I apply this quote today?

_____
_____
_____

Who else needs to hear this quote today?

_____
_____
_____

At the End of Your Day

What will I do differently going forward?

_____
_____
_____

Knowing what I now know, what I am grateful for today?

_____
_____
_____

"Believe you can and you're half way there."
-Theodore Roosevelt

Beginning Your Day

What does this quote mean to me today?

_____

_____

_____

How will I apply this quote today?

_____

_____

_____

Who else needs to hear this quote today?

_____

_____

_____

At the End of Your Day

What will I do differently going forward?

_____

_____

_____

Knowing what I now know, what I am grateful for today?

_____

_____

_____

"All that we are is the result of what we have thought." -Buddha

Beginning Your Day

What does this quote mean to me today?

_____

_____

_____

How will I apply this quote today?

_____

_____

_____

Who else needs to hear this quote today?

_____

_____

_____

At the End of Your Day

What will I do differently going forward?

_____

_____

_____

Knowing what I now know, what I am grateful for today?

_____

_____

_____

"You are not a drop in the ocean. You are the entire ocean, in a drop." -Rumi

Beginning Your Day

What does this quote mean to me today?

_____

_____

_____

How will I apply this quote today?

_____

_____

_____

Who else needs to hear this quote today?

_____

_____

_____

At the End of Your Day

What will I do differently going forward?

_____

_____

_____

Knowing what I now know, what I am grateful for today?

_____

_____

_____

"Don't let the fear of suffering limit your possibility." -Sadhguru

Beginning Your Day

What does this quote mean to me today?

_____

_____

_____

How will I apply this quote today?

_____

_____

_____

Who else needs to hear this quote today?

_____

_____

_____

At the End of Your Day

What will I do differently going forward?

_____

_____

_____

Knowing what I now know, what I am grateful for today?

_____

_____

_____

"It matters not how strait the gate, how charged with punishments the scroll, I am the master of my fate, I am the captain of my soul." -William Ernest Henley

Beginning Your Day

What does this quote mean to me today?

_____
_____
_____

How will I apply this quote today?

_____
_____
_____

Who else needs to hear this quote today?

_____
_____
_____

At the End of Your Day

What will I do differently going forward?

_____
_____
_____

Knowing what I now know, what I am grateful for today?

_____
_____
_____

"Don't be afraid to be different." -Michael Jackson

Beginning Your Day

What does this quote mean to me today?

_____
_____
_____

How will I apply this quote today?

_____
_____
_____

Who else needs to hear this quote today?

_____
_____
_____

At the End of Your Day

What will I do differently going forward?

_____
_____
_____

Knowing what I now know, what I am grateful for today?

_____
_____
_____

"If you do not make peace with your past, it will keep showing up in your present." -Wayne Dyer

Beginning Your Day

What does this quote mean to me today?

_____

_____

_____

How will I apply this quote today?

_____

_____

_____

Who else needs to hear this quote today?

_____

_____

_____

At the End of Your Day

What will I do differently going forward?

_____

_____

_____

Knowing what I now know, what I am grateful for today?

_____

_____

_____

"The only thing keeping you from what you want is your story about why you can't have it." -Tony Robbins

Beginning Your Day

What does this quote mean to me today?

_____

_____

_____

How will I apply this quote today?

_____

_____

_____

Who else needs to hear this quote today?

_____

_____

_____

At the End of Your Day

What will I do differently going forward?

_____

_____

_____

Knowing what I now know, what I am grateful for today?

_____

_____

_____

"In order to achieve something you have never achieved, you must do something you have never done." -Les Brown

Beginning Your Day

What does this quote mean to me today?

_____

_____

_____

How will I apply this quote today?

_____

_____

_____

Who else needs to hear this quote today?

_____

_____

_____

At the End of Your Day

What will I do differently going forward?

_____

_____

_____

Knowing what I now know, what I am grateful for today?

_____

_____

_____

"Whether you think you can or you think you can't, you're right." -Henry Ford

Beginning Your Day

What does this quote mean to me today?

_____

_____

_____

How will I apply this quote today?

_____

_____

_____

Who else needs to hear this quote today?

_____

_____

_____

At the End of Your Day

What will I do differently going forward?

_____

_____

_____

Knowing what I now know, what I am grateful for today?

_____

_____

_____

"If you really want to do something, you will find a way. If you don't, you'll find an excuse." -Jim Rohn

Beginning Your Day

What does this quote mean to me today?

_____
_____
_____

How will I apply this quote today?

_____
_____
_____

Who else needs to hear this quote today?

_____
_____
_____

At the End of Your Day

What will I do differently going forward?

_____
_____
_____

Knowing what I now know, what I am grateful for today?

_____
_____
_____

"There are two primary choices in life; to accept conditions as they exist, or to accept the responsibility for changing them." -Denis Whitley

Beginning Your Day

What does this quote mean to me today?

_____

_____

_____

How will I apply this quote today?

_____

_____

_____

Who else needs to hear this quote today?

_____

_____

_____

At the End of Your Day

What will I do differently going forward?

_____

_____

_____

Knowing what I now know, what I am grateful for today?

_____

_____

_____

"We see things not as they are, but as we are." -H.M. Tomlinson

Beginning Your Day

What does this quote mean to me today?

_____

_____

_____

How will I apply this quote today?

_____

_____

_____

Who else needs to hear this quote today?

_____

_____

_____

At the End of Your Day

What will I do differently going forward?

_____

_____

_____

Knowing what I now know, what I am grateful for today?

_____

_____

_____

"When you are going through hell, keep going."
-Winston Churchill

Beginning Your Day

What does this quote mean to me today?

_____
_____
_____

How will I apply this quote today?

_____
_____
_____

Who else needs to hear this quote today?

_____
_____
_____

At the End of Your Day

What will I do differently going forward?

_____
_____
_____

Knowing what I now know, what I am grateful for today?

_____
_____
_____

"Every next level of your life will demand a different you." -Leonardo DiCaprio

Beginning Your Day

What does this quote mean to me today?

_____
_____
_____

How will I apply this quote today?

_____
_____
_____

Who else needs to hear this quote today?

_____
_____
_____

At the End of Your Day

What will I do differently going forward?

_____
_____
_____

Knowing what I now know, what I am grateful for today?

_____
_____
_____

"Don't give up what you want most, for what you want now." -Richard G. Scott

Beginning Your Day

What does this quote mean to me today?

_____
_____
_____

How will I apply this quote today?

_____
_____
_____

Who else needs to hear this quote today?

_____
_____
_____

At the End of Your Day

What will I do differently going forward?

_____
_____
_____

Knowing what I now know, what I am grateful for today?

_____
_____
_____

"There is only one way to get anybody to do anything. And that is by making the other person want to do it." -Dale Carnegie

Beginning Your Day

What does this quote mean to me today?

_____
_____
_____

How will I apply this quote today?

_____
_____
_____

Who else needs to hear this quote today?

_____
_____
_____

At the End of Your Day

What will I do differently going forward?

_____
_____
_____

Knowing what I now know, what I am grateful for today?

_____
_____
_____

"For what it's worth: it's never too late to be whoever you want to be. I hope you live a life you're proud of. And if you find that you're not, I hope you have the strength to start over." -F. Scott Fitzgerald

Beginning Your Day

What does this quote mean to me today?

_____
_____
_____

How will I apply this quote today?

_____
_____
_____

Who else needs to hear this quote today?

_____
_____
_____

At the End of Your Day

What will I do differently going forward?

_____
_____
_____

Knowing what I now know, what I am grateful for today?

_____
_____
_____

"Stay away from negative people, they've got a problem for every solution." -Albert Einstein

Beginning Your Day

What does this quote mean to me today?

_____
_____
_____

How will I apply this quote today?

_____
_____
_____

Who else needs to hear this quote today?

_____
_____
_____

At the End of Your Day

What will I do differently going forward?

_____
_____
_____

Knowing what I now know, what I am grateful for today?

_____
_____
_____

"You can't go back and change the beginning, but you can start where you are and change the ending." -C. S. Lewis

Beginning Your Day

What does this quote mean to me today?

_____

_____

_____

How will I apply this quote today?

_____

_____

_____

Who else needs to hear this quote today?

_____

_____

_____

At the End of Your Day

What will I do differently going forward?

_____

_____

_____

Knowing what I now know, what I am grateful for today?

_____

_____

_____

"I hated every minute of training, but I said, suffer now and live the rest of your life as a champion." -Muhammad Ali

Beginning Your Day

What does this quote mean to me today?

_____
_____
_____

How will I apply this quote today?

_____
_____
_____

Who else needs to hear this quote today?

_____
_____
_____

At the End of Your Day

What will I do differently going forward?

_____
_____
_____

Knowing what I now know, what I am grateful for today?

_____
_____
_____

"To me, defeat in anything is merely temporary... Defeat simply tells me that something is wrong in my doing; it is a path leading to success and truth." -Bruce Lee

Beginning Your Day

What does this quote mean to me today?

_____

_____

_____

How will I apply this quote today?

_____

_____

_____

Who else needs to hear this quote today?

_____

_____

_____

At the End of Your Day

What will I do differently going forward?

_____

_____

_____

Knowing what I now know, what I am grateful for today?

_____

_____

_____

"You've got to practice the vibration of what you want until the vibration of your desire supersedes the vibration of doubt. And when the vibration of your desire supersedes the vibration of doubt, BAM! IT HAPPENS!" -Abraham Hicks

Beginning Your Day

What does this quote mean to me today?

_____
_____
_____

How will I apply this quote today?

_____
_____
_____

Who else needs to hear this quote today?

_____
_____
_____

At the End of Your Day

What will I do differently going forward?

_____
_____
_____

Knowing what I now know, what I am grateful for today?

_____
_____
_____

"People may not remember what you do or what you say but they will always remember how you made them feel." -Maya Angelou

Beginning Your Day

What does this quote mean to me today?

_____

_____

_____

How will I apply this quote today?

_____

_____

_____

Who else needs to hear this quote today?

_____

_____

_____

At the End of Your Day

What will I do differently going forward?

_____

_____

_____

Knowing what I now know, what I am grateful for today?

_____

_____

_____

"Where you are right now doesn't have to determine where you'll end up." -Barack Obama

Beginning Your Day

What does this quote mean to me today?

_____
_____
_____

How will I apply this quote today?

_____
_____
_____

Who else needs to hear this quote today?

_____
_____
_____

At the End of Your Day

What will I do differently going forward?

_____
_____
_____

Knowing what I now know, what I am grateful for today?

_____
_____
_____

"Your journey has molded you for your greater good, and it was exactly what it needed to be. Don't think that you've lost time. It took each and every situation you have encountered to bring you to the now. And now is right on time." -Asha Tyson

Beginning Your Day

What does this quote mean to me today?

_____
_____
_____

How will I apply this quote today?

_____
_____
_____

Who else needs to hear this quote today?

_____
_____
_____

At the End of Your Day

What will I do differently going forward?

_____
_____
_____

Knowing what I now know, what I am grateful for today?

_____
_____
_____

"I do not fix problems. I fix my thinking, then problems fix themselves." -Louise Hay

Beginning Your Day

What does this quote mean to me today?

_____

_____

_____

How will I apply this quote today?

_____

_____

_____

Who else needs to hear this quote today?

_____

_____

_____

At the End of Your Day

What will I do differently going forward?

_____

_____

_____

Knowing what I now know, what I am grateful for today?

_____

_____

_____

"You must find the place inside yourself where nothing is impossible." -Deepak Chopra

Beginning Your Day

What does this quote mean to me today?

_____
_____
_____

How will I apply this quote today?

_____
_____
_____

Who else needs to hear this quote today?

_____
_____
_____

At the End of Your Day

What will I do differently going forward?

_____
_____
_____

Knowing what I now know, what I am grateful for today?

_____
_____
_____

"The world breaks everyone. And afterward many are strong at the broken places." -Ernest Hemingway

Beginning Your Day

What does this quote mean to me today?

_____

_____

_____

How will I apply this quote today?

_____

_____

_____

Who else needs to hear this quote today?

_____

_____

_____

At the End of Your Day

What will I do differently going forward?

_____

_____

_____

Knowing what I now know, what I am grateful for today?

_____

_____

_____

"The future depends on what you do today."
-Mahatma Gandhi

Beginning Your Day

What does this quote mean to me today?

_____

_____

_____

How will I apply this quote today?

_____

_____

_____

Who else needs to hear this quote today?

_____

_____

_____

At the End of Your Day

What will I do differently going forward?

_____

_____

_____

Knowing what I now know, what I am grateful for today?

_____

_____

_____

"I want one moment in time when I'm more than I thought I could be; when all of my dreams are a heartbeat away, and the answers are all up to me." -Whitney Houston

Beginning Your Day

What does this quote mean to me today?

_____

_____

_____

How will I apply this quote today?

_____

_____

_____

Who else needs to hear this quote today?

_____

_____

_____

At the End of Your Day

What will I do differently going forward?

_____

_____

_____

Knowing what I now know, what I am grateful for today?

_____

_____

_____

"If it scares you, it might be a good thing to try." -Seth Godin

Beginning Your Day

What does this quote mean to me today?

_____

_____

_____

How will I apply this quote today?

_____

_____

_____

Who else needs to hear this quote today?

_____

_____

_____

At the End of Your Day

What will I do differently going forward?

_____

_____

_____

Knowing what I now know, what I am grateful for today?

_____

_____

_____

"The measure of who we are is what we do with what we have." -Vince Lombardi

Beginning Your Day

What does this quote mean to me today?

_____

_____

_____

How will I apply this quote today?

_____

_____

_____

Who else needs to hear this quote today?

_____

_____

_____

At the End of Your Day

What will I do differently going forward?

_____

_____

_____

Knowing what I now know, what I am grateful for today?

_____

_____

_____

"Fortune favors the bold." -Latin Proverb

Beginning Your Day

What does this quote mean to me today?

_____

_____

_____

How will I apply this quote today?

_____

_____

_____

Who else needs to hear this quote today?

_____

_____

_____

At the End of Your Day

What will I do differently going forward?

_____

_____

_____

Knowing what I now know, what I am grateful for today?

_____

_____

_____

"Love yourself like your life depends on it, because it does." -Anita Moorjani

Beginning Your Day

What does this quote mean to me today?

_____
_____
_____

How will I apply this quote today?

_____
_____
_____

Who else needs to hear this quote today?

_____
_____
_____

At the End of Your Day

What will I do differently going forward?

_____
_____
_____

Knowing what I now know, what I am grateful for today?

_____
_____
_____

"As I grow older, I pay less attention to what men say. I just watch what they do." -Andrew Carnegie

Beginning Your Day

What does this quote mean to me today?

_____
_____
_____

How will I apply this quote today?

_____
_____
_____

Who else needs to hear this quote today?

_____
_____
_____

At the End of Your Day

What will I do differently going forward?

_____
_____
_____

Knowing what I now know, what I am grateful for today?

_____
_____
_____

"If you hear a voice within you say 'you cannot paint,' then by all means, paint, and that voice will be silenced." -Vincent Van Gogh

Beginning Your Day

What does this quote mean to me today?

_____

_____

_____

How will I apply this quote today?

_____

_____

_____

Who else needs to hear this quote today?

_____

_____

_____

At the End of Your Day

What will I do differently going forward?

_____

_____

_____

Knowing what I now know, what I am grateful for today?

_____

_____

_____

"Being realistic is the most commonly traveled road to mediocrity." -Will Smith

Beginning Your Day

What does this quote mean to me today?

_____
_____
_____

How will I apply this quote today?

_____
_____
_____

Who else needs to hear this quote today?

_____
_____
_____

At the End of Your Day

What will I do differently going forward?

_____
_____
_____

Knowing what I now know, what I am grateful for today?

_____
_____
_____

"Think of yourself as a human magnet constantly attracting what you speak, think, and feel."
-Esther Hicks

Beginning Your Day

What does this quote mean to me today?

_____

_____

_____

How will I apply this quote today?

_____

_____

_____

Who else needs to hear this quote today?

_____

_____

_____

At the End of Your Day

What will I do differently going forward?

_____

_____

_____

Knowing what I now know, what I am grateful for today?

_____

_____

_____

"Nothing binds you except your thoughts; nothing limits you except your fear; and nothing controls you except your beliefs." -Marianne Williamson

Beginning Your Day

What does this quote mean to me today?

_____
_____
_____

How will I apply this quote today?

_____
_____
_____

Who else needs to hear this quote today?

_____
_____
_____

At the End of Your Day

What will I do differently going forward?

_____
_____
_____

Knowing what I now know, what I am grateful for today?

_____
_____
_____

"Life is 10% what happens to you and 90% how you react to it." -Charles R. Swindoll

Beginning Your Day

What does this quote mean to me today?

_____
_____
_____

How will I apply this quote today?

_____
_____
_____

Who else needs to hear this quote today?

_____
_____
_____

At the End of Your Day

What will I do differently going forward?

_____
_____
_____

Knowing what I now know, what I am grateful for today?

_____
_____
_____

"No price is too high to pay for the privilege of owning yourself." -Friedrich Nietzsche

Beginning Your Day

What does this quote mean to me today?

_____
_____
_____

How will I apply this quote today?

_____
_____
_____

Who else needs to hear this quote today?

_____
_____
_____

At the End of Your Day

What will I do differently going forward?

_____
_____
_____

Knowing what I now know, what I am grateful for today?

_____
_____
_____

"The greatest problems we have in life have nothing to do with our abilities, but rather the perceived limitations we place on ourselves that come from our own beliefs." -Kain Ramsey

Beginning Your Day

What does this quote mean to me today?

_____
_____
_____

How will I apply this quote today?

_____
_____
_____

Who else needs to hear this quote today?

_____
_____
_____

At the End of Your Day

What will I do differently going forward?

_____
_____
_____

Knowing what I now know, what I am grateful for today?

_____
_____
_____

"Too many of us are not living our dreams because we are living our fears." -Les Brown

Beginning Your Day

What does this quote mean to me today?

_____

_____

_____

How will I apply this quote today?

_____

_____

_____

Who else needs to hear this quote today?

_____

_____

_____

At the End of Your Day

What will I do differently going forward?

_____

_____

_____

Knowing what I now know, what I am grateful for today?

_____

_____

_____

"Turn your wounds into wisdom. You will be wounded many times in your life. You will make mistakes. Some people will call them failures. But I have learned that failure is just God's way of moving you in another direction." -Oprah Winfrey

Beginning Your Day

What does this quote mean to me today?

_____

_____

_____

How will I apply this quote today?

_____

_____

_____

Who else needs to hear this quote today?

_____

_____

_____

At the End of Your Day

What will I do differently going forward?

_____

_____

_____

Knowing what I now know, what I am grateful for today?

_____

_____

_____

"When you change the way you look at things, the things you look at change." -Wayne Dyer

Beginning Your Day

What does this quote mean to me today?

_____
_____
_____

How will I apply this quote today?

_____
_____
_____

Who else needs to hear this quote today?

_____
_____
_____

At the End of Your Day

What will I do differently going forward?

_____
_____
_____

Knowing what I now know, what I am grateful for today?

_____
_____
_____

"We are never more than a belief away from our greatest love, deepest healing, and most profound miracles." -Gregg Braden

Beginning Your Day

What does this quote mean to me today?

_____
_____
_____

How will I apply this quote today?

_____
_____
_____

Who else needs to hear this quote today?

_____
_____
_____

At the End of Your Day

What will I do differently going forward?

_____
_____
_____

Knowing what I now know, what I am grateful for today?

_____
_____
_____

"Your life is an accumulation of the choices you've made. Each choice starts a behavior that becomes a habit that has an impact on the compound effect of your life. Be conscious of your choices." -Darren Hardy

Beginning Your Day

What does this quote mean to me today?

_____
_____
_____

How will I apply this quote today?

_____
_____
_____

Who else needs to hear this quote today?

_____
_____
_____

At the End of Your Day

What will I do differently going forward?

_____
_____
_____

Knowing what I now know, what I am grateful for today?

_____
_____
_____

"Everything is rigged in your favor." -Rumi

Beginning Your Day

What does this quote mean to me today?

_____

_____

_____

How will I apply this quote today?

_____

_____

_____

Who else needs to hear this quote today?

_____

_____

_____

At the End of Your Day

What will I do differently going forward?

_____

_____

_____

Knowing what I now know, what I am grateful for today?

_____

_____

_____

"Follow your pain as if it were a candle in the night, leading you to a place of decision. " -Caroline Myss

Beginning Your Day

What does this quote mean to me today?

_____
_____
_____

How will I apply this quote today?

_____
_____
_____

Who else needs to hear this quote today?

_____
_____
_____

At the End of Your Day

What will I do differently going forward?

_____
_____
_____

Knowing what I now know, what I am grateful for today?

_____
_____
_____

"It's not the critic who counts; not the man who points out how the strong man stumbles, or where the doer of deeds could've done better. The credit belongs to the man who is actually in the arena, whose face is marred by dust and sweat and blood; who at best knows in the end the triumph of achievement, and who at worst, if he fails, fails while daring greatly, so that his place shall never be with those cold and timid souls who neither know victory nor defeat." -Theodore Roosevelt

Beginning Your Day

What does this quote mean to me today?

_____
_____
_____

How will I apply this quote today?

_____
_____
_____

Who else needs to hear this quote today?

_____
_____
_____

At the End of Your Day

What will I do differently going forward?

_____
_____
_____

Knowing what I now know, what I am grateful for today?

_____
_____
_____

"If you're not in the arena also getting your ass kicked, I'm not interested in your feedback." -Brene Brown

Beginning Your Day

What does this quote mean to me today?

_____
_____
_____

How will I apply this quote today?

_____
_____
_____

Who else needs to hear this quote today?

_____
_____
_____

At the End of Your Day

What will I do differently going forward?

_____
_____
_____

Knowing what I now know, what I am grateful for today?

_____
_____
_____

"When your self worth goes up, your net worth goes up." -Mark Victor Hansen

Beginning Your Day

What does this quote mean to me today?

_____

_____

_____

How will I apply this quote today?

_____

_____

_____

Who else needs to hear this quote today?

_____

_____

_____

At the End of Your Day

What will I do differently going forward?

_____

_____

_____

Knowing what I now know, what I am grateful for today?

_____

_____

_____

"Decide what you want. Believe you can have it. Believe you deserve it and believe it's possible for you. And then close your eyes and every day for several minutes, visualize having what you want, feeling the feelings of already having it. Come out of that and focus on what you are grateful for already and really enjoy it. Then go into your day and release it to the Universe and trust that the Universe will figure out how to manifest it." -Jack Canfield

Beginning Your Day

What does this quote mean to me today?

_____
_____
_____

How will I apply this quote today?

_____
_____
_____

Who else needs to hear this quote today?

_____
_____
_____

At the End of Your Day

What will I do differently going forward?

_____
_____
_____

Knowing what I now know, what I am grateful for today?

_____
_____
_____

"The beginning is the most important part of the work." -Plato

Beginning Your Day

What does this quote mean to me today?

_____
_____
_____

How will I apply this quote today?

_____
_____
_____

Who else needs to hear this quote today?

_____
_____
_____

At the End of Your Day

What will I do differently going forward?

_____
_____
_____

Knowing what I now know, what I am grateful for today?

_____
_____
_____

"If your actions inspire others to dream more, learn more, do more and become more, you are a leader." -John Quincy Adams

Beginning Your Day

What does this quote mean to me today?

_____

_____

_____

How will I apply this quote today?

_____

_____

_____

Who else needs to hear this quote today?

_____

_____

_____

At the End of Your Day

What will I do differently going forward?

_____

_____

_____

Knowing what I now know, what I am grateful for today?

_____

_____

_____

"What you don't forgive, you become." -Unknown

Beginning Your Day

What does this quote mean to me today?

_____

_____

_____

How will I apply this quote today?

_____

_____

_____

Who else needs to hear this quote today?

_____

_____

_____

At the End of Your Day

What will I do differently going forward?

_____

_____

_____

Knowing what I now know, what I am grateful for today?

_____

_____

_____

"Most of the important things in the world have been accomplished by people who have kept on trying when there seemed to be no hope at all." -Dale Carnegie

Beginning Your Day

What does this quote mean to me today?

_____

_____

_____

How will I apply this quote today?

_____

_____

_____

Who else needs to hear this quote today?

_____

_____

_____

At the End of Your Day

What will I do differently going forward?

_____

_____

_____

Knowing what I now know, what I am grateful for today?

_____

_____

_____

"You have to train your mind to be stronger than your emotions or you'll lose every time." -Sanchita Kar

Beginning Your Day

What does this quote mean to me today?

_____

_____

_____

How will I apply this quote today?

_____

_____

_____

Who else needs to hear this quote today?

_____

_____

_____

At the End of Your Day

What will I do differently going forward?

_____

_____

_____

Knowing what I now know, what I am grateful for today?

_____

_____

_____

"Anytime you feel negative emotion, stop and say: 'Something is important here, otherwise I would not be feeling this way. What is it that I want?' And then simply turn your attention to what you do want... In the moment you turn your attention to what you want, the negative attraction stops and the positive attraction begins. And your feeling will change from not feeling good to feeling good." -Esther Hicks

Beginning Your Day

What does this quote mean to me today?

_____
_____
_____

How will I apply this quote today?

_____
_____
_____

Who else needs to hear this quote today?

_____
_____
_____

At the End of Your Day

What will I do differently going forward?

_____
_____
_____

Knowing what I now know, what I am grateful for today?

_____
_____
_____

"There is freedom waiting for you, on the breezes of the sky and you ask, 'what if I fall'...Oh, but my darling, what if you fly?" -Erin Hanson

Beginning Your Day

What does this quote mean to me today?

_____
_____
_____

How will I apply this quote today?

_____
_____
_____

Who else needs to hear this quote today?

_____
_____
_____

At the End of Your Day

What will I do differently going forward?

_____
_____
_____

Knowing what I now know, what I am grateful for today?

_____
_____
_____

"I fear not the man who has practiced 10,000 kicks once, but I fear the man who has practiced one kick 10,000 times." -Bruce Lee

Beginning Your Day

What does this quote mean to me today?

_____

_____

_____

How will I apply this quote today?

_____

_____

_____

Who else needs to hear this quote today?

_____

_____

_____

At the End of Your Day

What will I do differently going forward?

_____

_____

_____

Knowing what I now know, what I am grateful for today?

_____

_____

_____

"I am only one, but, I am one. I cannot do everything, but, I can do something. And I will not let what I cannot do interfere with what I can do." -Edward Everett Hale

Beginning Your Day

What does this quote mean to me today?

_____
_____
_____

How will I apply this quote today?

_____
_____
_____

Who else needs to hear this quote today?

_____
_____
_____

At the End of Your Day

What will I do differently going forward?

_____
_____
_____

Knowing what I now know, what I am grateful for today?

_____
_____
_____

"You don't have to be great to start, but you have to start to be great." -Zig Ziglar

Beginning Your Day

What does this quote mean to me today?

_____
_____
_____

How will I apply this quote today?

_____
_____
_____

Who else needs to hear this quote today?

_____
_____
_____

At the End of Your Day

What will I do differently going forward?

_____
_____
_____

Knowing what I now know, what I am grateful for today?

_____
_____
_____

"The only way to do great work is to love what you do. If you haven't found it yet, keep looking. Don't settle." -Steve Jobs

Beginning Your Day

What does this quote mean to me today?

_____
_____
_____

How will I apply this quote today?

_____
_____
_____

Who else needs to hear this quote today?

_____
_____
_____

At the End of Your Day

What will I do differently going forward?

_____
_____
_____

Knowing what I now know, what I am grateful for today?

_____
_____
_____

"It doesn't matter how slowly you go, as long as you do not stop." -Confucios

Beginning Your Day

What does this quote mean to me today?

_____

_____

_____

How will I apply this quote today?

_____

_____

_____

Who else needs to hear this quote today?

_____

_____

_____

At the End of Your Day

What will I do differently going forward?

_____

_____

_____

Knowing what I now know, what I am grateful for today?

_____

_____

_____

"I don't believe in circumstances. The people who get on in this world are the people who get up and look for the circumstances they want, and, if they can't find them, make them." -George Bernard Shaw

Beginning Your Day

What does this quote mean to me today?

_____

_____

_____

How will I apply this quote today?

_____

_____

_____

Who else needs to hear this quote today?

_____

_____

_____

At the End of Your Day

What will I do differently going forward?

_____

_____

_____

Knowing what I now know, what I am grateful for today?

_____

_____

_____

"I learned that courage was not the absence of fear, but the triumph over it. The brave man is not he who does not feel afraid, but he who conquers that fear." -Nelson Mandela

Beginning Your Day

What does this quote mean to me today?

_____

_____

_____

How will I apply this quote today?

_____

_____

_____

Who else needs to hear this quote today?

_____

_____

_____

At the End of Your Day

What will I do differently going forward?

_____

_____

_____

Knowing what I now know, what I am grateful for today?

_____

_____

_____

"I have discovered in life that there are many ways of getting almost anywhere you want to go, if you really want to go." -Langston Hughes

Beginning Your Day

What does this quote mean to me today?

_____

_____

_____

How will I apply this quote today?

_____

_____

_____

Who else needs to hear this quote today?

_____

_____

_____

At the End of Your Day

What will I do differently going forward?

_____

_____

_____

Knowing what I now know, what I am grateful for today?

_____

_____

_____

"Instead of looking at the past, I put myself ahead twenty years and try to look at what I need to do now in order to get there." -Diana Ross

Beginning Your Day

What does this quote mean to me today?

_____
_____
_____

How will I apply this quote today?

_____
_____
_____

Who else needs to hear this quote today?

_____
_____
_____

At the End of Your Day

What will I do differently going forward?

_____
_____
_____

Knowing what I now know, what I am grateful for today?

_____
_____
_____

"Do the best thing that you can do right now from where you currently stand that makes you feel as good as you can possibly feel." -Abraham Hicks

Beginning Your Day

What does this quote mean to me today?

_____

_____

_____

How will I apply this quote today?

_____

_____

_____

Who else needs to hear this quote today?

_____

_____

_____

At the End of Your Day

What will I do differently going forward?

_____

_____

_____

Knowing what I now know, what I am grateful for today?

_____

_____

_____

"I have learned over the years that when one's mind is made up, this diminishes fear; knowing what must be done always does away with fear." -Rosa Parks

Beginning Your Day

What does this quote mean to me today?

_____

_____

_____

How will I apply this quote today?

_____

_____

_____

Who else needs to hear this quote today?

_____

_____

_____

At the End of Your Day

What will I do differently going forward?

_____

_____

_____

Knowing what I now know, what I am grateful for today?

_____

_____

_____

"On this journey, you never know what you are being prepared for." -Michelle Obama

Beginning Your Day

What does this quote mean to me today?

_____
_____
_____

How will I apply this quote today?

_____
_____
_____

Who else needs to hear this quote today?

_____
_____
_____

At the End of Your Day

What will I do differently going forward?

_____
_____
_____

Knowing what I now know, what I am grateful for today?

_____
_____
_____

"Don't find fault, find a remedy." -Henry Ford

Beginning Your Day

What does this quote mean to me today?

_____

_____

_____

How will I apply this quote today?

_____

_____

_____

Who else needs to hear this quote today?

_____

_____

_____

At the End of Your Day

What will I do differently going forward?

_____

_____

_____

Knowing what I now know, what I am grateful for today?

_____

_____

_____

"I don't have any time to stay up all night worrying about what someone who doesn't love me has to say about me." -Viola Davis

Beginning Your Day

What does this quote mean to me today?

_____

_____

_____

How will I apply this quote today?

_____

_____

_____

Who else needs to hear this quote today?

_____

_____

_____

At the End of Your Day

What will I do differently going forward?

_____

_____

_____

Knowing what I now know, what I am grateful for today?

_____

_____

_____

"If you want something really bad that means you're meant to have it. That's the way Spirit tells us why we're here. It sends us here wanting it..."
-Unknown

Beginning Your Day

What does this quote mean to me today?

_____

_____

_____

How will I apply this quote today?

_____

_____

_____

Who else needs to hear this quote today?

_____

_____

_____

At the End of Your Day

What will I do differently going forward?

_____

_____

_____

Knowing what I now know, what I am grateful for today?

_____

_____

_____

"Open your eyes and look within. Are you satisfied with the life you're living?" -Bob Marley

Beginning Your Day

What does this quote mean to me today?

_____

_____

_____

How will I apply this quote today?

_____

_____

_____

Who else needs to hear this quote today?

_____

_____

_____

At the End of Your Day

What will I do differently going forward?

_____

_____

_____

Knowing what I now know, what I am grateful for today?

_____

_____

_____

"When the world is silent, even one voice becomes powerful." -Malala Yousafzai

Beginning Your Day

What does this quote mean to me today?

_____
_____
_____

How will I apply this quote today?

_____
_____
_____

Who else needs to hear this quote today?

_____
_____
_____

At the End of Your Day

What will I do differently going forward?

_____
_____
_____

Knowing what I now know, what I am grateful for today?

_____
_____
_____

"When I dare to be powerful, to use my strength in the service of my vision, then it becomes less and less important whether I am afraid." -Audre Lorde

Beginning Your Day

What does this quote mean to me today?

_____

_____

_____

How will I apply this quote today?

_____

_____

_____

Who else needs to hear this quote today?

_____

_____

_____

At the End of Your Day

What will I do differently going forward?

_____

_____

_____

Knowing what I now know, what I am grateful for today?

_____

_____

_____

"The obstacles are showing you what you are resisting inside." -Deepak Chopra

Beginning Your Day

What does this quote mean to me today?

_____

_____

_____

How will I apply this quote today?

_____

_____

_____

Who else needs to hear this quote today?

_____

_____

_____

At the End of Your Day

What will I do differently going forward?

_____

_____

_____

Knowing what I now know, what I am grateful for today?

_____

_____

_____

"If you are silent about your pain, they will kill you and say you enjoyed it." -Zora Neale Hurston

Beginning Your Day

What does this quote mean to me today?

_____

_____

_____

How will I apply this quote today?

_____

_____

_____

Who else needs to hear this quote today?

_____

_____

_____

At the End of Your Day

What will I do differently going forward?

_____

_____

_____

Knowing what I now know, what I am grateful for today?

_____

_____

_____

"For things to change, YOU have to change. For things to get better, YOU have to get better. For things to improve, YOU have to improve. When YOU grow, EVERYTHING in your life grows with you." -Jim Rohn

Beginning Your Day

What does this quote mean to me today?

_____
_____
_____

How will I apply this quote today?

_____
_____
_____

Who else needs to hear this quote today?

_____
_____
_____

At the End of Your Day

What will I do differently going forward?

_____
_____
_____

Knowing what I now know, what I am grateful for today?

_____
_____
_____

"There is no better than adversity. Every defeat, every heartbreak, every loss, contains its own seed, its own lesson on how to improve your performance next time." -Malcolm X

Beginning Your Day

What does this quote mean to me today?

_____

_____

_____

How will I apply this quote today?

_____

_____

_____

Who else needs to hear this quote today?

_____

_____

_____

At the End of Your Day

What will I do differently going forward?

_____

_____

_____

Knowing what I now know, what I am grateful for today?

_____

_____

_____

"The starting point of all achievement is desire." -Napoleon Hill

Beginning Your Day

What does this quote mean to me today?

_____
_____
_____

How will I apply this quote today?

_____
_____
_____

Who else needs to hear this quote today?

_____
_____
_____

At the End of Your Day

What will I do differently going forward?

_____
_____
_____

Knowing what I now know, what I am grateful for today?

_____
_____
_____

"Look closely at the present you are constructing. It should look like the future you are dreaming." -Alice Walker

Beginning Your Day

What does this quote mean to me today?

_____
_____
_____

How will I apply this quote today?

_____
_____
_____

Who else needs to hear this quote today?

_____
_____
_____

At the End of Your Day

What will I do differently going forward?

_____
_____
_____

Knowing what I now know, what I am grateful for today?

_____
_____
_____

"People will love you. People will hate you. And none of it will have anything to do with you." -Esther Hicks

Beginning Your Day

What does this quote mean to me today?

_____

_____

_____

How will I apply this quote today?

_____

_____

_____

Who else needs to hear this quote today?

_____

_____

_____

At the End of Your Day

What will I do differently going forward?

_____

_____

_____

Knowing what I now know, what I am grateful for today?

_____

_____

_____

"Everything you've ever wanted is one step outside your comfort zone." -Jack Canfield

Beginning Your Day

What does this quote mean to me today?

_____
_____
_____

How will I apply this quote today?

_____
_____
_____

Who else needs to hear this quote today?

_____
_____
_____

At the End of Your Day

What will I do differently going forward?

_____
_____
_____

Knowing what I now know, what I am grateful for today?

_____
_____
_____

"A goal without a date is just a dream." -Milton H. Erickson

Beginning Your Day

What does this quote mean to me today?

_____

_____

_____

How will I apply this quote today?

_____

_____

_____

Who else needs to hear this quote today?

_____

_____

_____

At the End of Your Day

What will I do differently going forward?

_____

_____

_____

Knowing what I now know, what I am grateful for today?

_____

_____

_____

"Well behaved women seldom make history."
-Laurel Thatcher Ulrich

Beginning Your Day

What does this quote mean to me today?

_____

_____

_____

How will I apply this quote today?

_____

_____

_____

Who else needs to hear this quote today?

_____

_____

_____

At the End of Your Day

What will I do differently going forward?

_____

_____

_____

Knowing what I now know, what I am grateful for today?

_____

_____

_____

"I made a decision right then and there, whatever had or had not happened in the past, I was going to be the hero of my story." -Unknown

Beginning Your Day

What does this quote mean to me today?

_____

_____

_____

How will I apply this quote today?

_____

_____

_____

Who else needs to hear this quote today?

_____

_____

_____

At the End of Your Day

What will I do differently going forward?

_____

_____

_____

Knowing what I now know, what I am grateful for today?

_____

_____

_____

"The secret of your success is found in your daily routine. You will never change your life until you change something you do daily." -Darren Hardy

Beginning Your Day

What does this quote mean to me today?

_____

_____

_____

How will I apply this quote today?

_____

_____

_____

Who else needs to hear this quote today?

_____

_____

_____

At the End of Your Day

What will I do differently going forward?

_____

_____

_____

Knowing what I now know, what I am grateful for today?

_____

_____

_____

"In the end, we only regret the chances we didn't take." -Lewis Carroll

Beginning Your Day

What does this quote mean to me today?

_____

_____

_____

How will I apply this quote today?

_____

_____

_____

Who else needs to hear this quote today?

_____

_____

_____

At the End of Your Day

What will I do differently going forward?

_____

_____

_____

Knowing what I now know, what I am grateful for today?

_____

_____

_____

"You already have within you everything you need to turn your dreams into reality." -Wallace Wattles

Beginning Your Day

What does this quote mean to me today?

_____

_____

_____

How will I apply this quote today?

_____

_____

_____

Who else needs to hear this quote today?

_____

_____

_____

At the End of Your Day

What will I do differently going forward?

_____

_____

_____

Knowing what I now know, what I am grateful for today?

_____

_____

_____

"Do not wait. The time will never be just right. Start where you stand and work whatever tools you may have at your command. Better tools will be found as you go along." -Napoleon Hill

Beginning Your Day

What does this quote mean to me today?

_____
_____
_____

How will I apply this quote today?

_____
_____
_____

Who else needs to hear this quote today?

_____
_____
_____

At the End of Your Day

What will I do differently going forward?

_____
_____
_____

Knowing what I now know, what I am grateful for today?

_____
_____
_____

"Assume the feeling of your wish fulfilled. Feeling is the secret. " -Neville Goddard

Beginning Your Day

What does this quote mean to me today?

_____

_____

_____

How will I apply this quote today?

_____

_____

_____

Who else needs to hear this quote today?

_____

_____

_____

At the End of Your Day

What will I do differently going forward?

_____

_____

_____

Knowing what I now know, what I am grateful for today?

_____

_____

_____

"You can only move on if you accept that it's gone." -The Goddess Rebellion

Beginning Your Day

What does this quote mean to me today?

_____

_____

_____

How will I apply this quote today?

_____

_____

_____

Who else needs to hear this quote today?

_____

_____

_____

At the End of Your Day

What will I do differently going forward?

_____

_____

_____

Knowing what I now know, what I am grateful for today?

_____

_____

_____

"Let go of the old identities that no longer serve you. Who you were in the past is not who you are now. Step into your greatness." -Michael Stevenson

Beginning Your Day

What does this quote mean to me today?

_____
_____
_____

How will I apply this quote today?

_____
_____
_____

Who else needs to hear this quote today?

_____
_____
_____

At the End of Your Day

What will I do differently going forward?

_____
_____
_____

Knowing what I now know, what I am grateful for today?

_____
_____
_____

"Be brave with your life. Be fully who you are because there will never again be another you. Whatever struggle may come, live your life fearlessly." -Michelle Lynch

Beginning Your Day

What does this quote mean to me today?

_____
_____
_____

How will I apply this quote today?

_____
_____
_____

Who else needs to hear this quote today?

_____
_____
_____

At the End of Your Day

What will I do differently going forward?

_____
_____
_____

Knowing what I now know, what I am grateful for today?

_____
_____
_____

www.ingramcontent.com/pod-product-compliance
Lightning Source LLC
Chambersburg PA
CBHW060419290526
45791CB00002B/821